Trophy Bass Fishing

Ol' School & New

James C. Orr

authorHOUSE®

AuthorHouse™
1663 Liberty Drive
Bloomington, IN 47403
www.authorhouse.com
Phone: 1 (800) 839-8640

Published by AuthorHouse   02/04/2016

ISBN: 978-1-5049-6608-5 (sc)
ISBN: 978-1-5049-6609-2 (e)

Library of Congress Control Number: 2015920322

Print information available on the last page.

Any people depicted in stock imagery provided by Thinkstock are models, and such images are being used for illustrative purposes only. Certain stock imagery © Thinkstock.

This book is printed on acid-free paper.

Summary of "Trophy Bass Fishing, Ol' School & New"

The goal of this book is to provide a clear and concise understanding of catching trophy largemouth and smallouth bass without a lot of "fluff". Graphics and line charts that have been presented in many other bass fishing books were intentionally omitted. Many pictures were inputted to enhance text understanding, make the book entertaining, and an easy read. The format is to present some foundation information in each chapter followed by detailed tips and presentations in Sections V and VI.

The book begins with the concepts of *"critical thinking"*. The importance of safety on the water, the development of a trophy bass fisherman, the behavior of trophy bass, timing for trophies, and angler versatility are discussed.

Research and development is presented along with a discussion of rods, reels, lures, lines, and knots. How trophy largemouth and smallmouth bass respond to the various seasons are presented. The importance of record keeping and analysis is emphasized.

We then discuss catching trophy largemouth and smallmouth bass *on purpose*. This leads to the *master craftsman phase* of bass fishing i.e. planning for success, how water temps affects both species, good conservation practices, and the solunar influence on lunker bass. Fishing for trophy bass at night and during the cold-water periods are presented. An understanding that the angler must learn to fish off-shore for the trophies is emphasized.

Finally Sections V and VI provide detailed tips, lures, and presentations on how to catch trophy largemouth and smallmouth bass. These chapters use water temperatures as a guide to catch both species of bass during the spring, summer, fall, and winter seasons.

Lastly, the angler must understand that *right time, right place* and *right presentation* is the formula for success! This involves *critical thinking* and *attention to detail*. An angler must exercise patience and follow the process!!!

CONTENTS

Section V

Catching Trophy <u>Largemouth</u>

Section VI

Catching Trophy Smallmouth

Section VII

Summary

DEDICATIONS

There are three special individuals that have guided and inspired me as an angler and sportsman. They are Al Lindner, Doug Hannon and Homer Circle.

I have followed Al Lindner's programs, magazines, writings, and teachings for some 40+ years! He has made me a successful angler and a better person. Even today, Al constantly opens my eyes to new ways of catching bass by staying on the cutting-edge of the sport. He often reminds me that simple is sometimes best! Remembering some of his words have often "saved the day" on the water. Like Al, my favorite fish is the smallmouth bass.

The late, great Doug Hannon's knowledge of largemouth bass and how to catch lunker bass may never be duplicated. His accomplishments of catching hundreds of largemouth over 10 pound including many over 15 pound places him in a class by himself. His insights and reverence of the largemouth bass has taught me to always respect the fish and its environment. Like Doug, catching lunkers drives me every day on the water.

In my mind, Homer Circle will always be the greatest angling editor! His writings and angling knowledge have touched me throughout my life. His way of spinning a good yarn, injecting a good laugh, and still teaching how to catch bass was a wonderful skill. Often, the first article I would read would be "Uncle Homers"...Thank you Uncle Homer for all the good years you have shared with us...we miss you! Like Homer Circle, I hope to be bass fishing my last day on earth.

Sunset on Mullet Lake, Michigan
Special Recognition

I would like to thank my grandson, Tyler Frazier for the fishing memories we have shared…his first 3-pound largemouth on a jerkbait and his first 4-pound smallie on a swimming grub. Let's make some more memories Ty!

I also would like to thank all of the fishermen I have shared a boat with over the years. My hope is that your memories will last a lifetime as have mine!

Tyler was 8 years old when he caught this
3-pound largemouth on a jerkbait.

The author with a 7 pound 7 ounce smallie –
Lake Erie, April 2002 Lure: bladebait

INTRODUCTION

For the past several years an inner voice has told me to write a book on catching **trophy** *largemouth and smallmouth bass. That said, many of the words and chapters were composed in the night when I was trying to sleep! I could not rest until I put these words on paper...*

This is interesting because I have never written a book or article on bass fishing! I have been very fortunate to have lived and fished during the greatest decades of bass fishing. It is my privilege to share that journey with you.

Hello, my name is James Orr. Some of my friends gave me the nickname "Mr Bass" some 40-plus years ago. Since I was eight years old, bass fishing has been my passion! Even today, I can't wait to be back on the water chasing those ol' bass. Not just any bass, but lunker largemouth and smallmouth!

I've never had a TV show, haven't won the Bassmasters Classic or even written any articles or other books on bass fishing! I have no affiliations with any boat, rod, reel, lure manufacturers, fishing clubs, or organizations. Over the past 50 years I have spent thousands of hours fishing for bass in 21 states, Canada and Mexico. This has allowed me to meet and fish with many of the best anglers in the country and catch hundreds of largemouth over 7 pounds and hundreds of smallmouth over 5 pounds. It has also allowed me to fish many of the best waters for largemouth and smallmouth bass.

This book is not about me, but rather how becoming a complete bass angler will allow you to catch trophy bass *on purpose.* Part-time guiding over the past 40 years has completed me as I witness grown men act like little boys when they catch a true lunker. Teaching youths how to bass fish is a true honor and privilege. My hopes are that you can take from my experiences and tips found in this book so you to can make memories that last a lifetime. After all, there is still a little kid in all of us...

Best Wishes,
Mr Bass

Section 1

Critical Thinking

Chapter 1 Safety First!

Introduction

We often don't think about safety when we go bass fishing. Take it from me; this can be a *BIG MISTAKE!* I have had many "close calls" over the years. You should consider the time of year, weather forecast, waters you are fishing, the condition of the water (high/low/waves), who is in the boat with you (young, older, can't swim), and the number and condition of your life vests. *Don't let a tragedy ruin the day or someone's life!*

Use of Life Jackets

As Captain of the boat, you are responsible for the safety of your guests. Ask who can't swim. Many good swimmers have drowned in rough water conditions. While there are regulations requiring youths to wear life vests, you might consider someone wearing one at all times?

Have each person put their vests on *before* they get in the boat. Instruct each person not to stand or move around when you are under power. If you are fishing on a large lake (like the Great Lakes or Lake St. Clair) wear a life vest when you first notice white caps on the water (wind about 12 mph), even when you are fishing. Today's vests are light, comfortable, and easy to use. *DON'T TAKE CHANCES WITH SOMEONE'S LIFE!*

Do Your Homework Each Day

If you are fishing on a large lake, conditions often change quickly! A savvy Captain checks the weather report both in the evening and again the next morning before hitting the water. Knowing the current wind and wave conditions along with the forecast is imperative.

Once on the water, use Doppler Radar and carry a marine radio. Take your cell phone with you. I also purchase a Lake Erie towing service each year in case I get stranded or need assistance.

Water temps in the spring can be very dangerous if anyone falls in. Serious white caps and waves occur when winds get to 15+ mph. I move close to a ramp when this occurs and use one or two drift socks to slow and stabilize the boat. If conditions worsen you should get off the lake!

Mr Bass Tip: Raise the bow by trimming the motor up high and "plow the water" to navigate into the waves. Find the "sweet spot" that keeps the bow up and the water going by on both sides of the boat. Trying to plane off can easily spear a wave. Take your time and don't panic!

Watch the Skies!

In the spring of 2014, I was guiding a good friend for smallmouth on Lake Erie. Two other close friends in their boats chose to fish about 15 miles down the coastline. They were several miles from any ramp. The forecast was for severe isolated thunderstorms in the afternoon.

I decided not to fish down the lake (I wanted to) and stayed in a protected area only one mile from a protected marina. One of my friends called several times to get me to join them. Suddenly I noticed very dark skies approaching from the west. I could see the storm was moving very fast! I said to my friend "Let's get out of here!" We only got ½ mile when the storm hit us. Winds were 50+ mph with stinging hail. I could barely see to get to the marina.

When we got the boat tied up, I tried to call my friends down the lake to warn them of the approaching storm. NO ANSWER! They told me later that night that one of my friends left as soon as they saw the storm approaching. They decided to travel **with the storm** but had to travel 6 miles to a large marina. They just made it when the storm hit them.

Large, shallow lakes can become extremely dangerous very quickly!

My other friend and his two occupants decided to navigate **into the storm** because they were only two miles from their ramp. They couldn't make it in his 20-foot Skeeter bass boat! My friend told me the waves were 6 to 10 feet high. The boat filled with water even with two bilge pumps running. Waves were hitting them so hard, him and his two passengers were nearly thrown from the boat several times. They finally turned around and limped the seven miles with the storm to the other marina. Later that night, my friend told me he couldn't feel his hands or face and could barely walk! He said, "I thought we were going to die"!

Like me, my friend had 30+ years experience on Lake Erie. They were watching the storm approaching on Doppler Radar but misinterpreted the direction of the storm. They survived only through the grace of God!!

Even experienced fishermen can make mistakes. Stay close to marinas and ramps. Use a marine radio and heed the weather forecast.

Mr Bass Tip: If you are caught in a storm, never motor into the storm! Pull up on a protected sandy shore if available and get out of the boat. When navigating in high waves, move slowly and "ride the waves" and ALWAYS "WATCH THE SKIES"!!!

Chapter 2   Three Phases of Bass Fishing

Introduction

In the 50's and 60's there were three concepts that were often taught and discussed. The goal was to teach individuals to become highly knowledgeable and skilled at a certain skill or craft. These three phases are *apprentice, journeyman,* and *master craftsman.* As I look back at my fishing life it is obvious these phases also pertain to becoming a complete bass fisherman.

Apprentice Phase

The apprentice phase of bass fishing involves having an interest in fishing and catching bass in particular. This often begins with an already experienced and skilled fisherman introducing the sport or watching a fishing show on television. At this phase, ones knowledge and skill of bass fishing are very limited and usually required a significant period of time to advance to the journeyman phase.

Many fishermen stay at the apprentice level due to a lack of skillful teachings, limited time on the water, work/financial constraints, or health-limiting issues. I will discuss my apprentice phase as it pertains to bass fishing in much greater detail in Section II.

Journeyman Phase

A fisherman enters the journeyman phase of bass fishing when they no longer need a more experienced angler to catch bass. They have acquired the basic knowledge and skills to utilize various rods, reels, lines, and lures along with various presentation techniques to be successful.

The journeyman bass angler may have joined clubs and/or is fishing at various tournament levels. They usually are very skilled at certain techniques i.e. flipping & pitching, drop shotting, use of soft baits, topwaters, or hard baits etc. They are often skilled enough to win tournaments, be on pro staffs and even on television. Due to the nature of tournaments and clubs where the goal is to weigh in five bass each day, these anglers often only catch a lunker bass occasionally.

Many journeyman bass anglers don't get to plan their trips, select their lakes, or can only fish when they can get a day off from work. They are keenly aware of seasonal patterns, weather conditions, and the nature of the bass they pursue. They often don't get to apply moon phases, night fishing, or target lunker bass. Most of the fishermen I have met are tied to shore fishing (fish mostly visible cover) and don't understand off shore structure fishing. This is fine if this satisfies you as a bass angler. I will discuss my journeyman phase in much greater detail in Section III.

Master Craftsman Phase

Most bass fisherman never reach this phase. It can take a lifetime! This usually takes a combination of time on the water, exposure to many fishing lakes and conditions, experiences with other highly skilled anglers, record keeping/analysis, and *Critical Thinking!*

To me, the master craftsman phase means the bass angler is highly knowledgeable and skilled in many presentations and techniques. This allows them to plan for success, teach other anglers (professional guides), and quickly adapt to changing conditions.

They also possess a "sixth sense"; a sense of knowing what adjustments to make each day given the situation. A master craftsman angler also is very "open-minded" to different methods and techniques. *It is much better to be excellent at many presentations then an expert at just a few!* They also understand that catching trophy bass consistently is reaching the pinnacle of bass fishing. I will discuss this phase in much greater detail in Section IV.

Chapter 3 Location, Location, Location

Introduction

No, we are not talking about purchasing real estate! Perhaps the most difficult thing to learn and apply is how to find trophy bass! They can be in only 10% of the water or scattered at different depths and locations. Remember, the context of this book is how to catch lunkers. Big bass do things much differently then the smaller ones!

Have you ever heard the joke: "Where does a 500-pound gorilla sleep?" Answer: "Anywhere he wants to!" This also applies to trophy bass. They will spawn and live in the best locations of the area. They will also move much sooner than smaller bass and are usually in small groups and holding on somewhat isolated structure and cover.

If you are catching only smaller bass, you need to move to catch the lunkers! In other words, you **must fish differently** to catch them. **Many fishermen that I have fished with couldn't understand leaving fish to find bigger fish.** Yet, that is what you must do to find and catch trophy bass!

Deep, Shallow, or Somewhere In-Between?

This is my favorite concept in finding and catching trophy bass! I often say these words out loud while on the water! My fishing friend(s) for the day usually thinks it's just a joke and laughs, until I explain what those words mean to me.

These words remind me that the trophy bass can be anywhere at any given time of the day. That said, the lunkers are usually close to deeper water and the best structure/cover combination in the area. Deep water is a relative issue depending on what type of water you are fishing.

Largemouth and smallmouth bass are very different. They spawn at different temperatures, eat somewhat different prey, and are affected very differently by weather changes and seasonal patterns. The largemouth likes to ambush prey by hiding in the shadows of stumps, logs, and various weed types. The smallmouth bass spends a lot more time swimming and often prefers to chase down their prey. Deeper water, type of food sources, and key structure are important in understanding how to catch the trophies of each bass. I will discuss catching trophy largemouth and smallmouth in Sections V and VI.

That's a lot of water…where do I fish?

Clear natural lakes usually have a limited number of break lines before plunging into very deep water. They often have pronounced cover represented by various aquatic vegetation such as reeds, lily pads, coontail, hydrilla, milfoil etc. The trophy females move shallow only to spawn or actively feed. The deep weed line may be as deep as 22 feet in an ultra-clear lake. The trophies will usually relate to the deepest weeds and best food source. The deeper water in the lake along with irregular features (break lines or cover) is also often a key area to fish.

Reservoirs can be clear, stained, or muddy and usually have many break lines along with numerous creeks, points, and cover. Remember, deeper water close to spawning flats or points are the key for the lunkers.

The big bass often hold in creeks and ditches in spawning coves until they move up to spawn or feed.

I have limited experiences fishing rivers thus I will not discuss rivers in detail. River bass are usually much more shallow and use the current to ambush their prey. Please research books and DVDs on river bass fishing.

Mr Bass Tip: Start <u>Shallow</u> (2 to 8 feet) with fast and slow lures. These will be the most active fish. Then, check the <u>In-Between</u> depth (8 to 15 feet). Lastly, fish the <u>Deep</u> (15 to 25 feet). Trophy smallmouth bass can be much deeper!

Special note: See Sections V and VI on catching trophy largemouth and smallmouth bass.

<u>You Must be Versatile</u>

Learning to fish at different depths takes a personal commitment and understanding that the lunkers are only shallow to spawn and feed. Trophy largemouth are often holding at 15 to 25 feet deep. Trophy smallmouth are often at depths of 35 to 60 feet!

Many fishermen are tied to the shore and spend most of their day fishing visible cover. Thus, they are rarely coming in contact with trophy bass! This is why most trophy bass are caught during the pre-spawn/spawn! Use your electronics and lake maps to understand creeks, primary and secondary points, and spawning areas. Notice how the creeks and break lines relate to the shoreline features.

Now an understanding of the nature of the bass, prey relationship, seasonal patterns, and how the bass reacts to weather changes is imperative. Then you must factor in water temps, wind, sky conditions, and local patterns (contact bait stores & review tournament results). Lastly, the master craftsman considers the solunar influence along with major and minor feeding periods.

The complete angler must learn to fish at all depths to consistently catch trophy bass. Over my 50+ years I have learned what types of lures and presentations catch these lunkers. Selecting the correct lures and presentations will put those trophy bass in your boat! I will share my experiences with you in Sections V and VI.

Mr Bass Tip: Trophy bass don't just jump in the boat! They are difficult to pattern and catch. The details are very important. <u>YOU MUST BELIEVE IN THE PROCESS AND EXERCISE PATIENCE!!!</u> The number of bass you catch will go down considerably, but the memories and 'Bass of a Lifetime" are worth it!

Fish at Different Depths

Most bass fishermen are tied to the shore and visible cover. They are often weekend fishermen or just taking a youth(s) out for some bass fishing. They catch many bass in the shallows on soft plastics, hard baits, jigs, and topwater lures. Some of these fishermen could maximize their shallow success by selecting the best lures given the current conditions and seasonal patterns. We will examine this in detail in later chapters.

Early morning on the North Channel in Canada

Some fishermen have learned to fish shallow and offshore such as points, humps, isolated cover, and deep weed lines. They are often highly skilled in use of equipment, lures, and various presentations. They often catch bigger bass because fishing deeper puts their lures in contact with larger bass. Fishing this in-between water at the <u>right time</u>, in the <u>right place</u>, with the <u>right presentation</u> will put more lunkers in the boat. We will discuss this further in up-coming chapters.

Very few anglers have learned to fish in deep water (15 to 60 feet). Except for the spawning period and the short times lunkers are actively feeding, the true trophies are in these deep-water sanctuaries. Understanding this and learning how to fish in deep water is vital to catching trophy bass. We will also examine this in later chapters.

Chapter 4 Timing is EVERYTHING

Introduction

Catching trophy bass on purpose requires an in-depth knowledge of its nature, its prey and environment, and other factors such as fishing pressure. The successful angler is also a master in the use of rods, reels, hooks, lines, and lures. Once hooked, playing and handling these fish are vitally important. Another key to success is ***timing!***

It is very difficult to catch lunker bass right after the spawn, the passing of a cold front, when the water is rapidly falling, or during a fall "turnover". The big females are often caught during the pre-spawn when they are moving shallow to spawn.

**This 10 ½- pound largemouth was caught
on day of full moon in January!**
Lake Baccarac, Mexico

My experience is that the cold-water periods in spring and fall are key times for trophies. Another key time is the solunar major and minor feeding periods each day of the new and full moon in summer. Trophy bass can also be caught in winter on calm, sunny days. I will discuss all of this in greater detail in Sections V and VI.

The timing of fishing each lake when it is hot is vital. Establishing a network of fishing friends or bait shops to keep you current is recommended. Remember, on-line fishing reports are often days old or inaccurate.

One should research lakes to determine if they have produced trophy bass in recent years. Examples are: Dale Hollow doesn't produce 10-pound smallmouth any more yet it holds the world record of 11 pounds 15 ounces caught in 1955. It is difficult to catch a 6-pound smallmouth now on Lake St. Clair. Trophy largemouth catches on Falcon Lake and Lake Fork are down as of this writing due to fishing pressure. The introduction of zebra mussels and the round goby to the great lakes has caused the trophy smallmouth to spawn and live much deeper! Most lakes go through cycles of good and poor fishing. Point is, you must do your homework!

Trophy Bass & Smaller Bass

We have discussed that trophy and smaller bass are usually not found together and requires a different approach to catch and land the lunkers! Smaller bass will inhabit shallow, in-between and deep water. On the other hand, trophy bass are usually only in shallow water during the brief spawning period. They spend most of their time in mid-depths and deeper water. The only exception being shallow lakes with no deeper water available. Again, deep water is relative!

When the lunkers are actively feeding they will often patrol depths of 8 to 12 feet deep. In ultra-clear natural lakes the trophies will patrol the deep weed line that may be as deep as 22 feet! Thus, you should target these depths depending on the type of lake and cover that is in that particular lake.

This 9 pound 4 ounce trophy was holding on a small rocky point next to deep water. The air temp was 39 degrees that morning! She ate a jig-&-pig.

Studies have shown that some trophy bass patrol their area frequently while some stay at home on isolated cover. They are sometimes in small groups or by themselves.

Some are caught several times while others are never caught. If you only fish shallow most of the time you are not likely to catch many lunkers outside of the spawn.

When the trophies are actively feeding they are surprisingly easy to catch.

Of course *it's all about right time, right place, right presentation.* We will discuss how to catch these lunkers in Sections V and VI. I will also give you my tips for catching trophy bass during the prime times of each season.

What is Your Goal?

Many bass fishermen are quite happy to just spend the day on the water and catch any bass they can. If you are in a club or tournament the goal usually is to put five bass in the boat. With these approaches you are not likely to be fishing at the <u>right time</u>, <u>right place</u>, and <u>right presentation</u>. ***Your chances of catching a lunker bass are very limited!***

To catch trophy bass consistently one must think and fish differently! This is a decision you must make as an angler. Do you want numbers or trophies? I have memories when I have caught over 300 smallmouth in one day. ***But, I have memories of almost every lunker that my fishing partner or myself have caught in my lifetime!*** We don't have pictures of catching 300 bass. We have lots of pictures of catching trophy bass. It's all up to you...

***Bob caught this 9-pound plus trophy on our
trip to Lake El Salto, Mexico.
She hit a 10-inch, black & blue worm.***

Mr Bass Tip: The goal of this book is to teach you how to catch those lunkers! You WILL catch trophy bass by following my lifetime knowledge, tips, and techniques.

Special note: <u>YOU MUST BELIEVE IN THE PROCESS AND EXERCISE PATIENCE!!!</u>

Chapter 5 Records & Research

Introduction

In my early years I would occasionally catch a lunker. The problem was that I didn't have the knowledge and skill required to repeat that bass "high"! It finally occurred to me that I should be writing down all the factors related to the catch. After several years of recording my personal experiences I was able to repeat those trophy catches through data analysis and *critical thinking*!

Importance of Record Keeping

Recording the time/day/month, lake type, weather conditions, depth caught, lure used, presentation, and any special notes gave me valuable information to analysis and apply to each outing. A Study of Doug Hannon's life and angling success will validate the importance of record keeping. He was able to guarantee a lunker for his client(s) by carefully selecting his fishing days each month!

Importance of Research

Conducting research to catch trophy bass is a must! Watching bass fishing shows and tournaments on television will add to your knowledge base. Reading bass fishing books and articles (thanks Al and Uncle Homer) will further enhance your knowledge. My confidence and success soared as I applied these teachings to many different waters.

Today, my research includes in-depth study of maps, tournament results, lake history and cycle, current lake conditions, and a great network of angling friends across the country. Many pro anglers use lake flyovers to analysis the lake prior to a tournament. *The importance of keeping records and conducting research cannot be understated.* It can mean the difference between a poor or great fishing experience!

Data Overload

A cartoon came to mind one day on the water…Two bass fishermen are sitting in their 37-foot bass boat with twin 450 hp supersonic motors. The boat has a roll cage protecting the anglers and is equipped with bass-seeking radar. The driver is studying his 70-inch LCXX, reading his smart phone, checking the color selector, and reviewing the minute-by-minute fishing forecast.

Hours later he proclaims to his fishing partner whom has fallen asleep "The data indicates we should have been on the water at 5 a.m. down at the dam throwing a yellow crankbait! I'm waiting on the next update".

This could be a classic example of "data overload"!? It reminds me that the reason to fish is for the total experience; the wind, the water, the birds, sunrises and sunsets, the comradeship, and the pleasure of a day on the water. Capturing the quarry is secondary. Al Lindner reminds us "keep it simple"…

A great place to take a break and have lunch!

Section II

The Early Years

Chapter 1 Apprentice Phase

<u>Fishing Farm Ponds</u>

I grew up in small-farm country in southeastern Ohio. The fascination began when I watched some largemouth bass cruising the banks of one of the many farm ponds in the area. Being eight years old, them bass and me made a connection.

Fishing with crickets, worms, and grasshoppers only caught an occasional small bass. Those lunkers just kept swimming by and never gave me a second glance. One pond in particular was about 4 acres with many BIG bass. I would often watch those lunkers cruise in front of the cattails along the dam.

My first lure was a 3/8-ounce, yellow, single-blade spinnerbait. When spring began I threw that spinnerbait for hours along those cattails! No hits at first, but one day a BIG bass nailed that lure. The fight was on and I remember dragging that 5-pounder up the bank. Right then and there, I was hooked!! It has been all about trophy bass ever since!!!

3/8-ounce single-blade spinnerbait, Texas-rigged worm, 3/4-ounce black Jitterbug

Introduction to Worm Fishing

That spinnerbait caught several BIG largemouth over the next couple weeks. A couple of those bass went over 6 pounds. Suddenly, those bass would not touch that spinnerbait!

One evening in the summer I was throwing that spinnerbait along the dam when a man came down to the pond and started fishing. He was throwing something out into a cove that had a couple of small trees in the middle. To my amazement he was throwing the lure right into those trees!

As I watched, he suddenly snapped the rod back and a BIG bass jumped right out of those trees! I ran around the pond to check this out. That bass jumped 4 or 5 times before he finally landed her. He carefully unhooked the bass and knelt down to the water and released it.

He looked at me and said, "Would you like to try one of these?" He explained that it was a "Texas-rigged" plastic worm. The beauty being one could throw it into trees or weeds and it wouldn't hang up.

Well, he rigged one up for me and explained how to work the worm (I think it was black with a red tail?). In a few minutes I saw the line moving to the side. He shouted, "Set the hook"! That bass jumped 3 or 4 times and "spit" that worm right back at me! He laughed and told me that one has to "set-the-hook" just right not to lose the bass. Well, that did it, I was hooked again!!!

Breaking Thru

The spinnerbait and plastic worm were great lures but didn't always catch bass. I worked hard, saved some money and bought an "original" floating Rapala along with a black Jitterbug.

The floating Rapala caught many BIG bass by twitching or skipping it across the water. Sometimes, just letting it sit motionless brought violent strikes. Thinking back about fishing at night with that black Jitterbug still brings a smile to my face! I learned that one could catch many lunkers at night when they would not take a lure during the daytime. I noticed this was especially true during the full moon of summer.

These four lures landed many BIG bass over the next several years. My knowledge base grew considerably as I watched bass fishing shows and read every bass book in existence. I began to purchase many more lures and apply them to my pond fishing. ***My goal was to be a trophy bass fisherman.***

Section III

Research & Development Years

Chapter 1 Journeyman Phase

My first boat was an aluminum Bass Tracker from Bass Pro Shops. It was the early 70's when I drove 714 miles one-way to Springfield, Missouri to purchase that boat. It cost $3800, including flasher, trolling motor and 40 hp outboard. It was time for the next bass fishing phase...

Bass Fishing Shows & Articles

There were many great bass fishing anglers on television in the 70's and 80's. Many of these were famous guides and/or professional tournament anglers. Bass fishing magazines, books, and articles provided another wealth of information and knowledge. Anything involving catching trophy bass required dissecting and analysis. For me, bass fishing was "on fire"!

Bass fishing today has reached "data overload"! The sheer amount of information is overwhelming. One problem is that much of this information contradicts and confuses any novice trying to enter the sport. Pros are pushing their sponsors' boats, electronics, lures, lines, hooks, and anything else related to bass fishing. In my opinion, this is serving a great disservice to the novice wanting to enter the sport. Keeping it simple is hard to do!

Rods, Reels, Lines, & Knots

Fishing rods have reached the age of specialization! One would have you believe that you need graphite, fiberglass, and composite rods to be successful. Bass rods are many lengths along with many different tapers and actions. I caught hundreds of trophy bass on rods that would be considered inferior by today's standards. I recommend that you find an experienced bass fisherman that will keep rod selection simple and not break your pocketbook. One could be quite successful with two quality bait casting rods and one quality spinning rod.

Reels have gone down the same path as rods. The overall quality is very impressive compared to the reels of the 60's and 70's! Purchase two quality bait casting reels, one with a low-gear ratio and one with a high-gear ratio. This will adequately cover most bass fishing scenarios. One quality spinning reel will also suffice for most light-lure types/presentations. As you become a lot more experienced you will be able to select a specialized rod/reel combination without wasting a lot of money! This advice is offered because what rod or reel works for one bass fisherman may not work for you?

Fishing lines are also very specialized. Most of us can't agree on when to use mono, fluorocarbon, braid, or some "superline"! I try to keep this simple but it isn't easy. I use mono for most fishing applications (soft plastics, topwater, spinnerbaits, crankbaits). I use fluorocarbon for clear to ultra-clear water (mostly for smallmouth). I use braid for frogging or flipping into very dense mats so I can feel and set the hook better without breaking off. You may have to experiment to decide on your choice of rods, reels, and lines.

There are many knots one can use to tie to hooks or lures. Again, I try to keep this simple. Learn to tie the "double-improved clinch" and the "Palomar" knot for most applications. Both are essentially 100% knots. Use the "Loop", "Albright Special", and "Blood" knot for special applications. Use the "double-improved clinch" knot for braid with one modification. Wrap the tag end eight times around the standing line instead of five times.

Mr Bass Tip: Research and print "fishing knots" from the Internet. Study and practice each knot I mentioned. Keep a knot book in your boat for reference when you need it on the water. You will be glad you did!

Hard & Soft Baits

Most of the lures we use today to catch bass are in the categories of hard and soft baits. Hard baits are lures made from hard plastics, wood, and various metals. Examples are spinnerbaits, jerkbaits, crankbaits, most topwaters, jigs, bladebaits and umbrella rigs. One big advantage is their durability. They don't tear, dissolve, or fall apart and can last for many years. There is a time and place for hard baits that we will discuss later.

Soft baits are made from some type of soft plastics or rubber. Some examples are plastic worms, tubes, swimbaits, grubs, frogs, and creature baits just to name a few. The advantages of soft baits are their lifelike look, feel, and action. Bass will often hold onto a soft bait longer allowing the angler more time to set the hook. Some disadvantages are they tear, fall apart, discolor, and are ingested, sometimes killing the bass.

Catching trophy bass often requires the angler to chose the best hard or soft bait at that particular time! The water temperature, current weather conditions, type of lake, lake condition, and seasonal patterns are the main factors that affect this choice. Each day requires ***critical thinking*** to make the right adjustments.

Obviously a lunker is sometimes caught on most of these hard and soft baits. My records and on-water experiences indicate that only certain lures in these two categories ***consistently catch trophy bass.*** Of course, what lures catches lunkers in California lakes may differ considerably from lakes in Michigan! This is where local lake research comes into play. We will examine this in Sections V and VI.

Seasonal Patterns

Trophy bass are strongly influenced by the seasons. The seasons of spring, summer, fall, and winter can vary tremendously across the country. For instance, the spawn can be rather short in northern lakes while lasting several months in southern lakes. Summer fishing lasts much longer in southern waters. I use water temperatures as my guide to selecting the types of lures, presentations, and locations to catch trophy bass.

**Rex with a 6.75 lb. smallie caught in early
spring – his 1ˢᵗ 6 lb. bronzeback!**

Spring can be divided into three periods; pre-spawn, spawn, and post-spawn. Many lunkers are caught during pre-spawn across the country. Trophy smallmouth can be taken right after ice-out when the water temps will be in the lower 40s. The trophies will still be 25 to 40 feet deep and require a slow, vertical presentation. Bladebaits are the ***best choice*** at this time. Over the years, my friend Rex became the best bladebait fisherman that I have shared a boat with catching many lunkers with these lures!

Trophy largemouth start their journey to the shallows when the water temps hit the mid to upper 40s. Prime water temps to catch these trophies are 45°F to 65°F. They can be surprisingly shallow (1 to 3 feet) during early spring warming trends and can be taken on a variety of lures and presentations.

Regardless of the species of bass you are pursuing ***right time, right place, right presentation*** *is the formula for success!!! This also requires an "attention to detail" and "critical thinking" in everything involved in the* *process.* We will discuss all of this in much greater detail in up-coming chapters.

Author with 7-pound plus largemouth-
early spring on "clown" jerkbait

Largemouth usually begin spawning around 62°F to 65°F while smallmouth are about 58°F to 62°F. Theses temps can be 3- to 5-degrees colder in northern climates. ***A key to remember is that the lunkers move up on warming trends and pull back during cold fronts!*** I do not target the lunkers during the actual egg laying period or "bed" fish. Post-spawn is a difficult time to catch lunkers as the big females are resting up which may last up to two weeks.

Mr Bass Tip: Some of the biggest largemouth bass in a given lake are taken on the first warming trend in January or February. It is even better for trophies when the warming trend coincides with the full moon of that month!

Trophy largemouth and smallmouth spawn at somewhat different temps and bottom compositions. The trophies of each species also respond to different lures and presentations. We will examine these differences along with my tips in Sections V and VI on how to catch trophy largemouth and smallmouth bass.

I caught this 5 pound 8 ounce smallie in August! It was very hot that day!!

Summer can be divided into early summer, summer, and late summer. Early summer can also be a difficult period to catch a trophy bass. The big bass are resting from the rigors of spawning and transitioning to main lake points, creek channels, humps, islands, and old roadbeds. It is difficult to stay on them during this relatively short period.

Summer and late summer can be very good fishing. All types of lures and presentations will catch bass. I have caught many lunkers during these two periods by finding prime structure/cover and factoring in stable weather, moon phases, and major/minor feeding times. By following this approach, one can avoid the so-called "dog days of summer"!

I look at fall as two periods. The first period being a few weeks just before "turnover" and the second period a few weeks after turnover. As the surface water cools in fall it becomes more dense and heavy. The surface water starts mixing with the warmer water. This only lasts a few days but is a difficult time to predict from lake to lake! Bass fishing is usually terrible for up to two weeks. Move to another lake if you experience this!

Trophy bass can be caught during these two periods. I really like the second period after turnover as the big bass are feeding up for winter and seem to prefer the cooler water temps from 65°F down to 48°F for largemouth and down to 42°F for smallmouth. This is a great time to fish as often you have the lake to yourself! I have caught many trophy smallmouth when the water temps hits 55°F and down to about 42°F.

**Bob caught this 5-pound plus smallie in fall on a
jerkbait at a "Finger Lake" in New York State.**

Winter trophy bass can be caught but requires a true dedication that most fishermen don't possess. My experience is the best winter times for trophy bass are during short warming trends (1 to 3 days). Pick a calm and sunny day to target the lunkers with the best time of day being afternoons. Fish VERY SLOWLY with jigs, jerkbaits, or grubs for largemouths. Bladebaits are best for trophy smallmouth from water temps of 55°F down to 42°F. Again, fish slowly and close to the bottom!

Record Keeping & Analysis

Recording the details and analyzing the data is very important each time you catch a trophy bass. Consider recording date, time, water temperature, depth, lake type, water condition (clear/stained/muddy), weather conditions (sunny/cloudly/p-cloudly/windy/calm/rainy etc.), lure used, presentation, and any special notes (i.e. approaching cold front; location on lake etc.). As you analysis the data over time the discrete patterns will begin to emerge. This knowledge will give you the confidence to repeat the catch throughout the seasons!

Most fishermen believe this is a waste of valuable fishing time. This is understandable as many of us only get limited time to bass fish. One can become very skilled and catch many largemouth and smallmouth bass but will only catch an occasional true trophy without this in-depth knowledge.

Every big bass expert learned how to catch trophy bass through their personal experiences. Having data allows them to excel and be able to predict the best times to catch those lunkers. Doug Hannon is a perfect example of this fact. There are many myths that are often disproved by time on the water! It's all in the details!

Author with 11-pound plus largemouth - "slow-rolled" spinnerbait thru deep trees
Lake Baccarac, Mexico

Tied to the Shore

This is one of the most important concepts that a bass fisherman must overcome to consistently catch trophy bass. A lot of bass fishermen join clubs and/or fish in bass tournaments. The goal is to put five bass in the boat on any given day. The shallow bass are always the most active and easy to catch. Thus, the shallows is where most bass anglers fish. This is also where the most fishing pressure exists. Even many pro fishermen are not comfortable fishing offshore.

Learning to fish the deeper weed lines, points, humps, roadbeds, and creek channels will put your lures where the lunkers live. Use you maps and electronics to understand the break lines and structure on your lakes. Key areas are often where deeper water comes close to shallow flats and points. Good topo maps will indicate creek channels, points, humps, and old roadbeds. You must fish these areas to determine where the "sweet spots" are located (where the trophy bass hold and feed). *One must master offshore fishing to consistently put those lunkers in the boat!*

Bob caught this trophy smallie on a deep break in the middle of a large bay!

Section IV

Catching Trophies On Purpose

Chapter 1   Master Craftsman Phase

Achieving this level of bass fishing usually takes many years of teachings, on-the-water experiences, and ***critical thinking!*** Most of us don't have the time, resources, exposure to many different lakes, and dedication to target trophy bass.

One must also be a true sportsman and hold the bass in high esteem. This carries through each day on the water in personal commitment to bass protection and conservation. Flipping a bass into the boat to thrash around injures the bass and removes its protective slime. A good quality net should be used to land the lunkers (recommend rubber). Cameras and scales should be readily available to minimize time out-of-water.

We should not target the bass when they are on the beds as the eggs are quickly eaten when we remove the bass from their nest. The number of boats and tournaments should be tightly controlled so that too many bass don't die from excessive pressure and handling on any given lake. I have fished lakes that were "fished out" just from excessive pressure from a bass fishing club(s)! Catch-and-release has helped considerably, but we need to advance our thinking and consider other negative actions.

Steve caught this 5 ½-pound pre-spawn smallie on a crankbait

Plan for Success

Many lakes do not support high numbers of trophy bass. Research is the key before you decide the destination of your next bass fishing trip. Knowing when the pre-spawn begins on trophy largemouth lakes like Guntersville, Lake Fork, Falcon, Chickamauga, and California lakes, to name a few is imperative. Being one week too early or one week too late will probably be a let down.

Targeting trophy smallmouth of 6+ pounds requires knowing what waters they are currently being caught in along with the lures and presentations needed to be successful. Ten years ago, many 6-pound smallmouth were available on Lake St. Clair but hard to find as of this writing. *You must do your homework!*

Many bass magazines feature "hot" destinations for trophy largemouth and smallmouth bass. Use the Internet to research the lake. Acquire and study a good map of the lake. Contact fishing shops and bait stores on the lake. Talk to any bass'n buddies that have experience on that body of water.

**Fiberglass mount of my 12 pound 12 ounce
bass from Lake Baccarac, Mexico**

Fishing a lake in Mexico means a substantial cost and travel commitment. Knowing the best months for those trophies goes a long ways towards success. Some months are too hot or too wet on Mexican lakes. Research and planning allowed me to catch numerous trophies on my first trip to Lake Baccarac in 1997; the biggest bass weighing 12 pounds 12 ounces. No matter where my next bass fishing trip is, I plan ahead even if it's an outing with my 11-year-old grandson, Tyler!

Let Water Temps be Your Guide

Largemouth and smallmouth bass are cold-blooded fish. Their body temperature is very close to the water temperature that they inhabit. As the water temps rise, so does the bass's metabolism and activity. I have discovered that the water temperature can be an excellent guide in selecting the best lures and presentations throughout the seasons for trophy bass. The water temps that I am referring to are surface temps from the electronics mounted in a typical bass boat.

When the winter ice begins to break up, the water temp is 39°F. The first warming trend in January and/or February is an excellent time to catch some true trophy largemouths, often the biggest of the year in that given lake! The water temp may be 44°F to 50°F but the first day of a warming trend will bring the big females up. If this occurs around the full moon, *JACKPOT!!*

Water temps still in upper 40's when Bob caught this big smallie!

Right after ice-out is when I begin to target trophy smallmouth. Bladebaits are king when the water is cold (39°F to 48°F). They are usually still in deep water (25 to 40 feet) but will take a bladebait using a slow, close-to-the-bottom presentation. More on catching trophy smallmouth in later chapters.

Choosing the best lures and presentations based on water temps are very accurate for both bass species. What always trumps this approach is a cold front, quickly falling water temps, or quickly falling water levels. Cold, muddy water entering the lake is the ultimate curse for trophy largemouth! ***Stable or warming water temps are the key in the spring!*** I will detail my preferred lures and presentations for catching trophy largemouth and smallmouth in Sections V and VI.

Bass Handling/Conservation

The conservation of our lakes and trophy bass is vital for the future of quality bass fishing. We must understand that only a small percentage of the bass ever reach trophy size. Old photos from the 30's, 40's, and 50's indicate that a much higher percentage of trophies existed in our lakes then exists today.

I have witnessed dozens of big bass floating on the surface a few days after a major bass tournament. Some anglers take a lunker home to mount or to eat. Other trophy bass die from poor catch and handling practices. Our goal should be to protect the overall quality of our fisheries and precious resources.

*We **MUST** release 6-pounders if we want to catch 7-pounders!*

The number of tournaments and contestants should be reduced. I have been on lakes where three to six tournaments are being held on the same day! Not much fun for a day on the water with your grandson. The so-called "flipping" of bass into the boat should be discontinued. All tournament caught bass should be immediately weighed and released (paperless). I'm confident that the format of major bass tournaments could be revised to keep the viewing audience entertained and still immediately release the bass. My idea of catch-and-release is not hauling the bass around in a livewell for several hours, putting them in a bag, and then holding them up for the audience to applaud! No amount of ice and/or special chemicals will eliminate the cumulative stress and delayed mortality the bass is likely to experience!

Use a rubber net to land the trophy and wet your hands before handling the fish. Use both hands to hold the lunker in a horizontal plane. Have a camera, scales, and tape measure handy to capture the moment if a mount is desired. Graphite or fiberglass mounts produce a high-quality product that lasts for years. Any trophy bass should not be eaten and should be immediately released! ***The "high" an angler gets when releasing a trophy bass to be caught by another lucky angler cannot be measured!***

Chapter 2   Solunar Bass Fishing

Introduction

It is amassing that many excellent bass anglers do not believe the moon phases along with the Major and Minor feeding periods each day have a significant influence on trophy bass! The late Doug Hannon, also known as "The Bass Professor" was able to predict and guarantee a trophy largemouth catch for his client(s)! Even some pro anglers argue that Doug's accomplishments were because he fished in the relatively shallow waters of Florida. *I beg to differ with them!!!*

Do You Believe?

My personal experiences are that the full and new moon phases plus the Major/Minor feeding periods **will put many more trophy bass in your boat.** This solunar influence seems to only work during *certain seasons.* My records indicate that the *full moon* of a <u>warming trend in the months of January and February</u> are key for lunker largemouth in reservoirs across the country.

Fishing the full and new moon periods are very effective once the trophy largemouth have transitioned to the main lake after spawning. This is a reliable pattern throughout the summer months up to early fall. I was able to predict trophy largemouth catches on *full moons of summer* for over 20 years *by fishing at night.* More on night fishing later.

When the water temps reach around 60°F in spring the smallmouth move onto shallow flats in huge waves to spawn on the first full moon. The males come in first to make the beds. The big female bass will be holding in deeper water close to these flats waiting on just the right time to come in and deposit her eggs. *Note: If conditions are not optimal, the big smallies will hold their eggs and spawn later, sometimes over a three-month period. If you are only catching 1- to 3-pound smallies (buck bass), move to deeper water nearby!*

*Special note: It is important to note that the **full moon** in January and/ or February needs to be associated with a warming trend. The full and new moon periods during summer are much more influential on a 2- to 3-day stable weather pattern. **The solunar effect does not seem to be significant during post-spawn, the transition period to the main lake (pre-summer), or during fall and winter.***

Trust the Process!

Sometimes as anglers we don't believe in something because we have not experienced it ourselves. Reading "Hannon's Field Guide for Bass Fishing" convinced me that the solunar influence on lunker largemouth bass was real. "The Original Moon Clock by Doug Hannon" copyright 1983 became a valuable tool that put many trophy bass in my boat. When an "excellent period" (major) occurred during the one-hour before sunset or one-hour before sunrise, the lunker bass were always active. ***You must be on a lunker spot on the lake when this period occurs!***

8 pound 6 ounce largemouth on the <u>day of a new moon in June</u>

The "Major" periods occur approximately every 12 hours and are called "moon overhead" and "moon underfoot". Good fishing can last up to two hours but can be shorter based on local weather conditions.

A "Minor" period also occurs every 12 hours but is 6 hours between the two majors in a 24-hour period. Good fishing can last up to 45 minutes but sometimes doesn't seem to occur at all? *There are no guarantees when it comes to bass fishing!* I use the "Solunar Calendar" printed in each issue of In-Fisherman for my bass fishing trips.

Mr Bass Tip: Some of the biggest largemouth bass in a given lake are taken on the first warming trend in January or February. It is even better for trophies when the warming trend coincides with the <u>full moon</u> of that month!

9 pound 8 ounce bass caught on the <u>day of full moon in February!</u>

Special note: My records indicate the <u>three nights/days before</u> the full and new moon were much more productive than the <u>three night/days after</u> each moon phase.

Chapter 3   Night Fishing for Trophy Bass

As the summer season comes in each year many anglers lose contact with the trophy bass. The true giants in any lake environment will take up the best food and structure/cover locations. Finding these key locations is vital! Many anglers call the heat of the summer the "dog days" meaning that fishing is usually poor. *They couldn't be further from the truth! I have caught many trophy largemouth and smallmouth in the month of August! You just need __right time__, __right place__, __right presentation!__*

This 7 ½-pound largemouth was caught __1 night before the full moon__ in August! It was also during a __major feeding period__ on a North Carolina lake.

Fishing at night is not for the faint of heart or the disorganized angler. Safety is also a major concern. One should know the lake intimately before attempting to navigate at night. Idling is recommended over running at high speeds. Black lights help the angler to see while fishing. Check local regulations for after-dark navigation requirements.

During the summer months the trophy largemouth are relating to main lake structure such as points, humps, underwater ridges, old roadbeds, deep-water islands, and creek channels. Use a good topo map and your electronics to find these key locations. These are the structures and locations to target for trophy largemouth at night.

The "sweet spots" to fish will usually be where deeper water touches or comes very close to the structure. Locating cover such as trees, stumps, rock piles, and deep weeds on these sweet spots is even better! Large flats with deep weed lines are also key lunker areas. ***Look for the irregular deep weed line features that are close to the deepest water in the area!*** I will share my lures of choice along with preferred presentations for trophy largemouth in Section V.

Trophy smallmouth in summer are relating to deep structure break lines, deep weed lines, scattered weed clumps, large isolated boulders, and humps surrounded by deep water. Trophy smallmouth will feed at night on the full and new moon. They will come to the surface and hit topwater lures. Another nighttime pattern is large spinnerbaits along deep weed lines and sharp structure break lines. I will share my lures of choice along with preferred presentations for trophy smallmouth in Section VI.

Night fishing for trophy largemouth and smallmouth is fun and very rewarding. You will have the lake to yourself and be very surprised how many lunkers are actively feeding at night during the summer season. An extra bonus is the night sounds of frogs, owls, foxes, calls of loons, and calls of whip-err-wills. Fishing under the bright stars and full moon is a surreal experience!

Mr Bass Tip: The lake needs to have clear to ultra-clear water for night fishing to be productive. Lakes that have high traffic from boaters, skiers, and jet skis are the best for night fishing!

Chapter 4   Fishing the Cold Water Periods

This 6 pound 10 ounce smallie was taken on a bladebait 3 days after ice-out. The trophy bass was 38 feet deep with the water temp at 42°F!

The two cold-water periods of each year are my favorite times to catch trophy largemouth and smallmouth. The first is early spring when the water first starts warming and the second is right before and after *turnover* in fall. Both species are active and feeding during these cold-water periods. Often, this is when you will catch the biggest lunkers of that year.

Trophy largemouth can be taken on warming trends in January/ February. As the water warms and pre-spawn begins the big females are moving into coves and small creeks where they are staging in preparation for the up-coming spawn. The water temps will be 44°F and warming to approximately 62°F to 65°F when spawning begins.

Trophy smallmouth can be taken right after ice-out when the water may be only 42°F. They will still be deep (25 to 40 feet on the Great Lakes) but will hit slow, vertical presentations. As water temps rise to the high 40's, they will make periodic forays to the shallows and feed. They can be taken with many lures/presentations during the pre-spawn. They will move up and drop back (always have suitcases packed) until spawning begins at approximately 58°F. Some trophy smallmouth will spawn as shallow as 5 feet, but 10 to 20 feet is much more common. ***Thus, it is best to target the depths of 10 to 25 feet for the pre-spawn giants!*** I will reveal my lures and presentations of choice for trophy largemouth and smallmouth during the cold-water periods in Sections V and VI.

Use bladebaits to catch trophy smallies right after ice-out

Chapter 5   Understanding Off-shore Fishing

Most bass fishermen fish shallow water and visible cover. The shallow fish are the most active and can be caught with many lures and presentations. These are also the most pressured fish. We have already discussed that the true monster bass are in deeper water and on off-shore structure except for the short spawning period.

A good topographical map will indicate multiple break lines that lead to deeper water. Other structural features such as humps, creek channels, old roadbeds, rock piles, cribs, and isolated boulders are often identified. These are all key features that will hold trophy bass assuming there is a food source and good cover available.

Two or more break lines that come close together and then drop off into much deeper water *and* makes contact with a secondary or main lake point will attract trophy bass. Off shore underwater humps, shoals with weeds, or isolated boulders will also attract these trophies.

**Creek channel was about 80 feet from
shoreline. Where would you fish?**

Depending on the lake type, trophy largemouth will hold on the deep weed line in natural lakes or the previously mentioned structure in reservoirs. When lunker largemouth are actively feeding they are often 8 to 12 feet deep. When they are neutral (not active but can be caught) they are often 15 to 25 feet deep.

Trophy smallmouth are often found on the same types of structure but usually much deeper. They will spend a good part of the season 35 to 60 feet deep if it is available. Smallmouth like deep humps, isolated boulders, break lines with sharp breaks, and transition areas where rock goes to sand. On the great lakes they will often be found loosely associated with large schools of baitfish. On Lake St. Clair (shallow lake) they can be found in 15 to 20 feet of water on small humps and/or isolated weed clumps.

One must learn to find and effectively fish these off-shore structures and cover to consistently catch trophy largemouth and smallmouth!

Bob with a 6-pound plus smallie! They are deep, shallow, or somewhere in-between!

Section V

Catching Trophy Largemouth

Chapter 1 The Nature of Trophy Largemouth

As we have discussed, trophy largemouth (7-pound plus) behave quite differently than the smaller bass. They will come in first in January/February after the cold weather period to feed. They often spawn earlier than smaller bass. They will usually be found on the ***best structure/cover that has a good food source!*** Lunker largemouth are often solitary and are attracted to isolated lay-down trees, stumps, rocks, and weed clumps. ***This is key cover to target during pre-spawn!***

The big females are usually only shallow to spawn (3 to 8 feet). They spend most of their time in depths of 8 to 12 feet when actively feeding (short periods) and 12 to 25 feet when they are neutral or inactive. Understanding when they are deep, shallow, or somewhere in-between is key to your success!

Trophy largemouth are highly affected by cold fronts, quickly falling water, quickly falling water temperatures, and cold/muddy water entering the lake. They will hide in dense weeds or mats, suspend off of key structure, or go deep and sulk on the bottom. No matter where they go, the lunkers ***are very difficult to catch when any of these occur!***

My jig & pig for pre-spawn largemouth is black/
blue with a blue chunk trailer

Chapter 2 Spring Fishing

Spring fishing for trophy bigmouths begins with the first warming trends in January or February. Unless of course, if your lake is frozen over. I use water temps in the spring to select the best lure(s) and presentation(s). **The following are my *tips* for pre-spawn trophies:**

Water temp: 42°F to 50°F

Mr Bass Tip #1: My lures at these water temps are: Jig & pig, jerkbaits

Presentation: *Use a 1/4- or 1/2-ounce jig, <u>black with blue strands</u> with a <u>blue</u> chunk trailer. Cast to small rocky points, lay-down logs, stumps, and drop-offs* **close to deep water.** *Fish jig <u>slowly</u> with light shaking and/or dragging presentation. If the line jumps or moves off, SET THE HOOK HARD WITH QUICK UPWARD SNAP OF ROD and keep reeling (no slack)!*

This is my cold-water jerkbait for off-color water (clown color)

Presentation: *Use a large jerkbait in colors <u>silver/black</u> for ultra/clear water and <u>clown</u> for off-color water. Fish <u>slowly</u> with twitch/twitch pause then twitch pause. Change the cadence to see what the fish want. Fish jerkbaits on edges of large spawning flats, secondary lake points, and creeks/ditches going into coves.*

Water temp: 50°F to 57°F

Mr Bass Tip #2: My lures at these water temps are: Lipless crankbaits, crankbaits, and jerkbaits

Special note: *This is a "<u>special time</u>" for lipless crankbaits (Rat-L-Traps)!! I have caught many lunkers up to 9 ½- pounds with this pattern.*

This 9 ½-pound bass hit a 3/4-ounce
<u>*Tennessee Shad*</u> *lipless crankbait.*

Presentation: *Use a <u>3/4-ounce lipless crankbait</u> in a <u>Tennessee Shad</u> color for clear to stained water and <u>gold</u> or <u>chartreuse</u> in muddy water. Use slow-speed reel (5.2:1) and erratic, stop-in-go retrieve. I often replace the factory* *hooks with high quality round bend hooks. Try to cause a lure deflection by bumping rocks, stumps, logs etc.*

    Presentation: *Use medium-diving crankbait in <u>shad</u> color for ultra-clear water and <u>firetiger</u> for stained & muddy water.* **<u>Fish the four corners of riprap on every bridge on the lake! Try to deflect the crankbait off underwater rocks with multiple casting angles. This is a MAJOR prespawn pattern at these water temps!!!</u>**

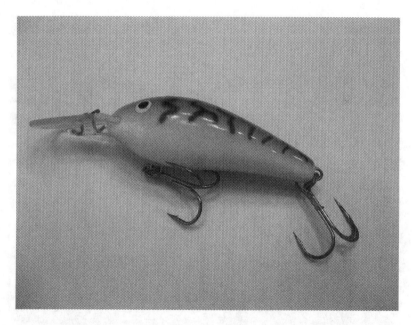

Medium-diving "firetiger" crankbait for bridge riprap

    Presentation: *Same as Tip #1 for jerkbaits*

Water temp: 58°F to 62°F

    Mr Bass Tip #3: My lures at these water temps are; Spinnerbaits (best), lipless crankbaits, crankbaits

    Special note: *58°F is the "**<u>magic</u>**" water temperature for spinnerbait fishing, especially if it's windy!*

Presentation: *Use a 1/2-ounce spinnerbait in <u>shad colors</u> for clear water and <u>chartreuse & white</u> for off-color water. I like a double-willowleaf (large blade <u>gold</u> & small blade <u>silver</u>) spinnerbait. Use a slow-speed reel (5.2:1) with an erratic retrieve (slow, stop & flutter, pull etc.)*

Presentation: *Same as Tip #2 for lipless crankbaits*

Presentation: *Same as Tip #2 for crankbaits*

1/2-ounce double-willowleaf spinnerbait for 58°F water temp

Water temp: 62°F to 66°F

Mr Bass Tip #4: My lures at these water temps are: Buzzbaits (best), Carolina-rigged lizards, lipless crankbaits

Special note: *A buzzbait is awesome when the **<u>water temp first hits 65°F on the spawning flats.</u>** "Power fish" a 1/2-ounce <u>white</u> buzzbait starting at 62°F thru 65°F water temps!!! Wait until you feel the <u>weight of the bass before setting the hook!</u> I have used this pattern all day and caught dozens* *of trophies on buzzbaits all over the country!!! **TARGET THE SPAWNING FLATS!***

    *Presentation: Use a 1/2-ounce <u>white</u> buzzbait with <u>shad</u> color skirt. Use 3/0 trailer hook and don't "peg" the hook with a plastic keeper over the eyelet! Put the trailer hook on first and then a small piece of plastic tubing on main hook shank so the trailer hook moves freely (trailer hook needed because sometimes the lunkers just "slap" at the lure)! "Power fish" and throw the buzzbait as far as you can to cover a lot of water. Use a high-speed reel (7.1:1 & up) with a steady retrieve. Braid or heavy mono (15 to 20-pound-test) line is best. This is a very short period of time so you must be on the lake every day to monitor the water temps on the flats. **<u>MAJOR PATTERN - HANG ON & HAVE FUN!</u>***

This 7-pound plus bass hit a white buzzbait on a spawning flat

    *Presentation: Use Carolina-rigged lizard with 1/2-ounce egg sinker and glass beads. I like 6- to 7-inch lizards in <u>watermelon seed</u> or <u>green pumpkin</u> colors. I usually use fluorocarbon line in 12 to 15-pound- test. **Target the spawning flats.** Just throw a long ways on a 7- to 8-foot medium-heavy rod* and drag it back slowly. For some reason **<u>big bass can't stand a lizard at spawning time!</u>**

Presentation: *Same as Tip #2 for lipless crankbaits*

<u>Water temp: 68°F to 72°</u>

Special note: *I stop fishing for the trophies during spawn and post-spawn! I <u>never fish for a lunker on a bed!</u> I wait for the summer period to arrive to resume targeting the trophy bass.*

Chapter 3   Summer Fishing

Summer fishing for trophy largemouth begins when the big females have rested and transitioned to the main lake. This usually occurs 2 to 3 weeks after spawning has ended. Key areas are main-lake points, creek channels, old roadbeds, deep-water islands, ridges, underwater humps, deep-water trees, and deep weed lines. *The" sweet spots" will be where break lines drop sharply into deeper water <u>and</u> come close to or touch these areas!*

*<u>Key to my success is fishing the</u> **full** <u>and</u> **new moon periods*** along with the **two half-moon days of each month** during the summer season. I also target the ***Major/Minor periods*** of each day. **The following are my *tips* for summer trophies:**

Special note: *Fish the <u>three preceding nights</u> and the <u>night</u> of the **full moon** each month. Fish the <u>three preceding days</u> and the <u>day</u> of the **new moon** each month. Fish the two half-moon days of each month during the daytime.*

Mr Bass Tip #5: <u>MY LURES FOR NIGHT FISHING ARE:</u> *Plastic worms, buzzbaits, Pop-Rs, Jitterbug, and spinnerbaits*

***This 7-pound plus bass hit a big black/blue
worm at night on a deep weed line.***

Special note: *Fish topwater lures and spinnerbaits over deep weeds (power fish)* **<u>during the major periods</u>** *when the lunkers are active at night!*

Presentation: *Use 8- to 12-inch worms (<u>black with blue tail</u> or any dark color i.e<u>. junebug/tequila sunrise/red shad</u>). Texas-rig with 1/4-ounce worm weight and sharp worm style hook. Fish worm* **slowly** *on edge of weeds (leave worm in place and shake worm) or on structures/cover mentioned above. When a hit or pick-up is detected SET THE HOOK WITH A QUICK UPWARD SNAP OF THE ROD and maintain pressure on the bass (no slack).*

"Power fish" black buzzbait over deep weeds
during "major" periods at night!

Presentation: *Use 1/2-ounce <u>black</u> buzzbait, <u>dark</u> colored Pop-R, <u>black</u>, 3/4- ounce Jitterbug, or <u>black</u>, 1/2-ounce spinnerbait with large single Colorado/Indiana blade (<u>black</u>, <u>red</u>, or <u>gold</u> blade color). Fish these lures during the <u>Major</u> feeding periods (I usually alternate these lures).* **Use plastic worms all other times.**

Presentation: *Use a slow steady retrieve with a buzzbait, Jitterbug, or spinnerbait so the lunkers can track and follow the vibrations to the lure (BIG BASS have very advanced lateral lines).*

Presentation: *Work the Pop-R slowly sometimes letting it sit still for several seconds. <u>Don't jerk until you feel the weight of the bass when fishing a buzzbait or Pop-R!</u>*

Mr Bass Tip #6: <u>MY LURES FOR DAYTIME FISHING ARE</u>:
Plastic worms, deep-diving crankbaits, jig & trailer

`Bruce caught this 9-½ pound trophy at sunset __1__
__day before the new moon in July__ on a plastic worm.
It was also a __"major"__ feeding period!

Presentation: Use 8- to 12-inch worms in __watermelon seed__, __green__
__pumpkin__, or __pumpkinseed__ colors (other colors may work based on water clarity).
Texas-rigged with 1/4- to 1/2-ounce worm weight and sharp worm style hook.
Fish worm slowly on deep weed line or on structures/cover mentioned above.
When a hit or pick-up is detected SET THE HOOK WITH A QUICK
UPWARD SNAP OF THE ROD and maintain pressure on the bass (no
slack).

Presentation: Use deep-diving (12 to 20 feet) crankbaits in __shad__, __blue/__
__chartreuse__, or __crawdad__ patterns for clear and ultra-clear water. Use __firetiger__
and __gold__ colors for off-color water. Throw crankbaits along deep weed lines,
ridges, humps, old roadbeds, and creek channels targeting 10 to 20 feet deep
water.

Presentation: Use 1/2- to 3/4-ounce __grass jigs__ (weighted end comes
to point) in __brown__ or __green pumpkin__ colors. Tip jigs with plastic craws,

swimbaits, or creature baits in <u>brown</u> or <u>green</u> hues. **TARGET THE DEEP WEED LINE!**

   Special note: *Deep weed lines may be as deep as 22 feet in ultra-clear and clear natural lakes or man-made impoundments.* **THIS IS A KEY SUMMER PATTERN FOR BIG BASS ON NATURAL LAKES AS DEEP WEEDS ARE OFTEN THE ONLY BIG BASS COVER! You may need a 1-ounce or bigger jig?**

Chapter 4   Fall Fishing

Fall fishing for trophy bass can be highly rewarding or somewhat frustrating! The big bass want to come up and feed before winter but the ever-changing weather can make contacting the lunkers difficult. Another problem is the fall "turnover" which only takes two to four days to occur but fishing is very poor for around two weeks after the turnover!

The up side of fall bass fishing is the changing of the leaves, cooler days and nights, and often having the lake virtually to yourself! Because of the fall turnover, I break fall bass fishing into two periods. The first period is _before turnover_ and the second period being _after turnover._ Again, **I use water temps to select my best lures and presentations for trophy bass during the fall.**

Special note: *As the water temps decrease with much cooler nights and daytime temperatures the baitfish migrate into creeks and to the back of coves. Use medium-diving crankbaits, lipless crankbaits, spinnerbaits, buzzebaits, and swimming jig & swimbait trailer to follow this migration. Look for baitfish flipping on the surface!*

Water temp: 72°F down to 65°F

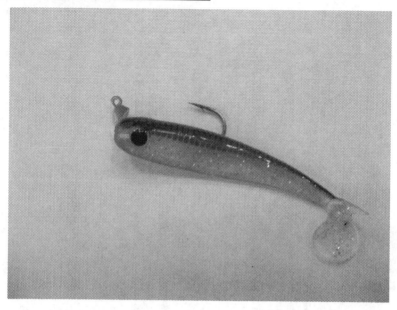

Swimming jig & swimbait trailer (shad patterns)

Mr Bass Tip #7: My lures at these water temps in <u>fall</u> are: Plastic worms, crankbaits, and swimming jig & trailer

Presentation: Same as Tip # 6 for plastic worms

*Presentation: Same as tip # 6 for crankbaits except add <u>**medium-diving crankbaits for water depths of 8 to 12 feet**</u>*

Presentation: Use swimming jig and swimbait trailers in <u>shad</u> colors. Swim jig by isolated weed clumps, deep weed edges, and along deeper water break lines close to shore (steeper banks).

Water temp: 65°F down to 62°F

Mr Bass Tip #8: My lures at these water temps in <u>fall</u> are: Topwaters, worms, crankbaits, swimming jig & trailer

"Power fish" a 1/2-ounce buzzbait on steep banks & deep weed lines

Presentation: *Use <u>white,</u> 1/2-ounce buzzbait, prop baits (Boy Howdy/ Devils Horse/Tiny Torpedo etc.), or Zara Spooks in <u>chrome</u> or <u>shad colors</u>, over deep weeds, weed clumps, or isolated cover (logs/trees/rocks) on <u>deeper break lines close to shore and secondary points going into coves.</u>*

Presentation: *Same as Tip #7 for crankbaits <u>**except use shad colors and fish steeper banks in main coves where baitfish are present!**</u>*

Presentation: *Same as Tip # 7 for swimming jigs & trailer <u>**except target steeper banks in main coves where baitfish are present!**</u>*

Special note: *If **"turnover"** occurs bass will suddenly become inactive. It often takes up to two weeks for feeding to resume!*

<u>Water temp: 58°F down to 55°F</u>

Mr Bass Tip #9: My lures at these water temps in <u>fall</u> are: Spinnerbait (best), crankbaits, swimming jig, chatterbaits

Use 1/2-ounce double-willowleaf (both blades silver is best) spinnerbait in shad patterns when water temp is 58°F.

Presentation: Use 1/2-ounce double-willowleaf spinnerbait (large blade silver, small blade silver) with shad color skirt. Fish steeper banks back in coves and any isolated cover i.e. lay down trees/logs, deep-water stumps, standing trees, rock out-croppings, and the **outside weed lines.**

Presentation: Same as tip #8 for crankbaits

Presentation: Same as Tip #8 for swimming jigs

Presentation: Use 3/8- or 1/2-ounce chatterbait and shad color skirt. Target deep weed lines and steeper banks with isolated cover. Use an erratic retrieve and flutter (drop) lure along cover.

Chapter 5   Winter Fishing

Winter fishing for trophy largemouth is truly for the dedicated bass fisherman. Safety is a concern as falling into water temps in the 40's can be fatal. The reward is that one can catch the **BIGGEST BASS IN THE LAKE** during the winter period!

The big bass in winter will move to the break lines close to the **_deepest water in that area_** of the lake. *They will be very lethargic due to water temps in the 40's. You **must fish slowly** to be successful. This is when close to-the-bottom and vertical presentations shine!* **Pick calm, sunny days and fish late morning thru early evening say; 11 a.m. to 4 p.m.** *Again, I use water temps to select the best lures and presentations for winter bass.*

Swimming jig with watermelon or green pumpkin swimbait trailer

Water temp: 55°F down to 50°F

Mr Bass Tip #10: My lures at these water temps in <u>fall</u> are: Crankbaits, lipless crankbaits, swimming jig, chatterbaits

Presentation: *Use medium-diving crankbaits in <u>shad and chrome colors and fish steeper banks in main coves where baitfish are present!</u> Target isolated cover (trees/stumps/logs/rocks) and deep weed lines.*

Presentation: *Use a <u>1/2-ounce lipless crankbait</u> in a <u>chrome</u> color for clear to stained water and <u>gold</u> or <u>chartreuse</u> in muddy water. Use slow-speed reel (5.2:1) and erratic, stop-in-go retrieve. I often replace the factory hooks with high quality round bend hooks.*

*Use 1/2-ounce chrome lipless crankbait-
look for baitfish in backs of creeks*

Presentation: *Use swimming jigs and swim bait trailers in <u>shad or green patterns.</u> Target isolated cover (trees/stumps/logs/rocks) and deep weed lines.*

Presentation: Use 3/8- or 1/2-ounce chatterbait and <u>shad</u> color skirt. Target deep weed lines and steeper banks with isolated cover. Use an erratic retrieve and flutter (drop) lure along cover.

Water temp: 50°F down to 42°F

Mr Bass Tip #11: My lures at these water temps are: Bladebaits (best), football jig & trailer, jerkbaits

Presentation: Use 1/2-ounce <u>silver</u> or <u>gold</u> bladebaits and **target 15 to 25 foot depths!** Use vertical presentation by lifting bladebait for vibration and then drop lure back down on <u>semi-tight line.</u> They will usually hit it on the fall or just as you start to pick it up. **<u>Fish from the lake bottom up 10 inches!</u>**

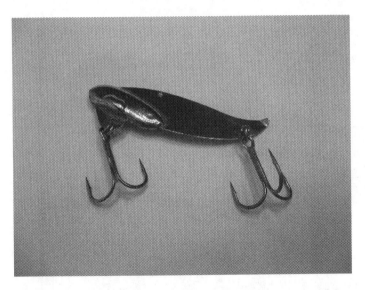

Bladebaits catch BIG BASS when the water is cold.

Presentation: Use 1/2- to 3/4-ounce football jigs (<u>brown </u>or <u>green</u>) with <u>brown, green,</u> or <u>black</u> strands and tipped with craw or creature bait trailers **<u>Target 12 to 25 feet depth on steep banks and channel breaks</u>**.

Presentation: Use deep-diving suspending jerkbaits in shad or chrome patterns. **Target steep banks and creek channel breaks. Fish lure slowly with short jerks and long pauses.**

Section VI

Catching Trophy Smallmouth

Bob caught this 6-½ pound smallie on a jerkbait - what a trophy!

Chapter 1   The Nature of Trophy Smallmouth

Trophy smallmouth are quite different then trophy largemouth. Cold fronts don't "shut down" BIG smallies. In fact, cold fronts often turn smallmouth on. Trophy smallmouth don't stay at home and always seem to have their "suitcases packed"! They spawn in 10 to 20 feet of water and are often 35 to 60 feet deep in summer!

Trophy smallies will school by class size after spawning (summer, fall, & winter). If you are only catching 2- to 4-pounders, you need to relocate! Usually the answer is "**_go deeper or locate better structure_**". You are usually doing the right things when you catch a 5-pound plus bronzeback!

To catch a 5-, 6-, or 7-pound smallmouth one **must fish in waters that have these trophies in sufficient numbers.** This requires research. My favorites for trophy smallmouth are the Great Lakes, Michigan lakes, New York lakes, and the Boundary Waters. What one will always appreciate about catching smallmouth is their "never-give- up attitude"!

*Mr Bass Tip #1: Many of the large bays of the Great Lakes hold MONSTER SMALLIES. Research these bays for **right time**, **right place**, **right presentation!!!***

Chapter 2   Spring Fishing

Spring fishing for trophy smallmouth begins a few days after ice-out. This is usually late March or early April in the waters I mentioned. I use water temps in the spring to select the best lure(s) and presentation(s). **The following are my *tips* for pre-spawn trophies:**

Water temp: 42°F to 48°F

Mr Bass Tip #2: My lures at these water temps are: Bladebaits, deep-diving jerkbaits

A <u>RARE</u> 7-pound plus smallie caught on a bladebait at 37 feet deep!

Presentation: *Use 3/4- to 1-ounce <u>silver</u>, <u>pearl</u>, or <u>gold</u> bladebait. Use a small cross-lock snap in the center hole (if there are three) on the bladebait. I usually put high quality split rings and round bend hooks on my bladebaits.*

Use 10 to 12-pound-test fluorocarbon line and a vertical presentation. **<u>Fish from the lake bottom up six inches. Lift the lure just enough to get vibration and drop on a semi-tight line.</u>** *The bass usually hits the lure on the fall or as you begin to lift the bait off the bottom.* ***TARGET GOOD STRUCTURE AT 25 TO 40 FEET DEEP!***

05/08/2014

Deep-diving jerkbaits catch BIG smallies, as Bob can attest!

Presentation: *Use a deep-diving suspending jerkbait in natural patterns. Use a small cross-lock snap to allow quick lure changes. Make a long cast back behind the boat and set trolling motor on 40 %. Let more line out, engage the spool and use jerk, jerk, pause; jerk, pause with rod tip held close to water surface. This is a Great Lakes technique called "strolling" (learned from the Pennsylvania boys). Use 8 to 10-pound- test fluorocarbon line to get lure as deep as possible.* ***TARGET GOOD STRUCTURE AT 15 TO 35 FEET DEEP!***

Special note: *Use a rubber net to land trophy smallmouth and handle bass carefully! Have camera and scales handy to minimize the out-of-water* *timeframe. A 6-pound smallie may be 20 years old, so RELEASE that trophy to be caught another day!*

Water temp: 49°F to 54°F

*Mr Bass Tip #3: My lures at these water temps are: **Bladebaits, deep-diving jerkbaits, crankbaits***

*Presentation: Use a 1/2- to 5/8-ounce <u>silver</u>, <u>pearl</u>, or <u>gold</u> bladebait. Use a small cross-lock snap in the center hole (if there are three) on the bladebait. I usually put high quality split rings and round bend hooks on my bladebaits. Use 10 to 12-pound-test fluorocarbon line and a vertical presentation. **<u>Fish from the lake bottom up six inches. Lift the lure just enough to get vibration and drop on semi-tight line.</u>** The bass usually hits the lure on the fall or as you begin to lift the bait off bottom. **TARGET GOOD STRUCTURE AT 17 TO 30 FEET DEEP AS THE BIG BASS WILL BE MOVING IN!***

*Presentation: Same as Tip # 1 for deep-diving jerkbaits **except target 17 to 30 foot depths!***

05/13/2014

Smallmouth feed on crayfish when the water temps are in the mid- 50's

Presentation: Use <u>medium-diving</u> crankbait in <u>crawdad</u> patterns on 12-pound-test fluorocarbon line. Use erratic retrieve and occasionally bump the lake bottom with the lure. **TARGET GOOD STRUCTURE AT 10 TO 12 FEET DEEP!**

Water temp: 55°F to 58°F

Mr Bass Tip #4: My lures at these water temps are: Deep & medium-diving jerkbaits, crankbaits, tubes, lipless crankbaits

Presentation: Use a deep-diving suspending jerkbait or medium-diving suspending jerkbait in natural patterns. Use a small cross-lock snap to allow quick lure changes. Make a long cast back behind the boat and set trolling motor on 40 %. Let more line out, engage the spool and use jerk, jerk, pause; jerk, pause with rod tip held close to water surface. This is a Great Lakes technique called "strolling" (learned from the Pennsylvania boys). Use 8 to 10-pound-test fluorocarbon line to get lure as deep as possible. **TARGET GOOD STRUCTURE AT 10 TO 20 FEET DEEP!**

Medium-diving suspending jerkbait

Special note: Use "strolling" presentation for deep-diving jerkbaits in 13 to 20 foot depths. <u>Cast</u> medium-diving jerkbaits in 10 to 13 foot depths with same retrieve.

Presentation: *Use <u>medium</u>-diving crankbait in <u>crawdad</u> patterns on 12-pound-test fluorocarbon line. Use erratic retrieve and occasionally bump the lake bottom with the lure. **TARGET GOOD STRUCTURE AT 10 TO 12 FEET DEEP!***

Presentation: *Use 1/4- to 1/2-ounce tube jigs. Use tubes in <u>green</u> and <u>brown</u> hues with <u>gold</u> or <u>red </u> or <u>purple</u> flakes. Drift with tubes bumping lake bottom. Set hook with quick upward snap of rod and maintain pressure (no slack). **TARGET GOOD STRUCTURE AT 10 TO 20 FEET DEEP!***

Target good structure at 7 to 12 feet with lipless crankbaits

Presentation: *Use 1/2-ounce lipless crankbait in a <u>chrome </u>finish. Use high-speed reel (7.1:1 & up) and erratic, stop-in-go retrieve. I often replace the* *factory hooks with high quality round bend hooks.* ***TARGET SCATTERED ROCKS & BOULDERS AND/OR SHOALS AT 7 TO 12 FEET DEEP!***

Water temp: 58°F to 62°F

Mr Bass Tip #5: My lures at these water temps are: Medium-diving crankbaits, tubes, lipless crankbaits, swim jig & grub

Special note: *As the big smallies get close to spawning they will suddenly stop hitting jerkbaits, crankbaits, tubes, and lipless crankbaits and become very selective!* ***It will seem like the bass are gone...*** *When this happens use a 1/4- to 1/2-ounce swimming jig rigged with a five-inch curly tail grub in colors <u>pearl</u> (best), <u>greens</u> or <u>purple.</u> Rig grubs with hook exposed. Make long casts and use slow steady retrieve. The smallies will track the grub and inhale it much like a walleye bite (learned this presentation from Al Lindner TV show).* ***TARGET SCATTERED ROCKS & BOULDERS AND/OR SHOALS AT 7 TO 15 FEET DEEP!***

3/8- ounce swim jig with 5- inch curly-tail grub

Presentation: *Same as Tip # 3 for medium-diving crankbaits.*

Presentation: *Same as Tip # 3 for tubes.*

Presentation: *Same as Tip # 3 for lipless crankbaits.*

Special note: *I stop fishing for the trophies during spawn and post-spawn! I <u>never fish for a lunker on a bed!</u> I wait for the summer period to arrive to resume targeting the trophy bass.*

Chapter 3 Summer Fishing

After spawning the trophy smallmouth (5-pounds & up) begin transitioning to summer haunts. They will rest for about two weeks and be very difficult to catch. Many five-pound smallies will stop at 20 to 25 feet deep for a period of time. The bigger smallmouth continue to move deeper to depths of 35 to 60 feet if available. **The following are my *tips* for trophy smallmouth during the summer season:**

Mr Bass Tip #6: My lures and presentations for summer trophy smallmouth are: Crankbaits, tubes, drop shot, topwater

Bruce caught this 6-pound smallie in July at 37 feet deep

*Special note: Many 5-pound smallies are available at 20 to 25 foot depths on deep-diving crankbaits and drop shot presentations. The 6-pound plus smallies are usually at 35 to 60 feet and seem to prefer tubes versus drop shot methods. **TARGET ISOLATED BOULDERS, DEEP WATER HUMPS,***

AND GOOD STRUCTURE FOR 6-POUND PLUS SMALLIES AT 35 FEET AND DEEPER WITH TUBES!

Presentation: *Use deep-diving crankbaits in <u>clear</u>, <u>shad</u>, and <u>crawdad</u> patterns. Use erratic stop-&-go retrieve on 10 to 12-pound-test fluorocarbon line.* **TARGET DROP-OFFS (break lines) AT 15 TO 25 FEET DEEP!**

Presentation: *Use 1/2- to 1-ounce tube jigs. Use tubes in <u>green</u> and <u>brown</u> hues with <u>gold</u> or <u>red</u> or <u>purple</u> flakes (use magnum flipping tubes for heavier jig weights). Drift with tubes bumping lake bottom (may need to long-line if windy)? Use drift sock(s) to slow and control boat if windy. Set hook with quick upward snap of rod and maintain pressure (no slack).* **TARGET GOOD STRUCTURE, DEEP WATER HUMPS, AND/OR ISOLATED BOULDERS AT 20 TO 60 FEET DEEP!**

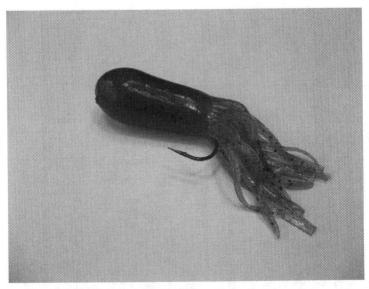

*Magnum flipping tube with 3/4 or 1-ounce
tube jig for depths of 35 to 60 feet*

Presentation: *Use drop shot presentations and adjust weight based on depth and wind (I like soft bait above weight about 8- to 10-inches). Use 7- to 8-foot medium action spinning rod and reel with 6- to 10-lb. test fluorocarbon line. Many drop shot baits will catch smallmouth; experiment with lure type,* *size, and color.* ***TARGET GOOD STRUCTURE, DEEP WTER HUMPS, AND/OR ISOLATED BOULDERS AT 20 TO 60 FEET DEEP!***

   Special note: *6-pound plus smallies rarely hit drop shot presentations? Use tubes for monster smallies during the summer season!*

   Special note: *Trophy smallmouth will hit <u>topwater lures</u> early and late in the day in water depths up to 40 feet during post-spawn, summer, and fall! Lakes with high boat traffic during the summer are prime topwater lakes at <u>night</u> on the <u>full</u> and <u>new</u> moon. These lunkers can be taken over deep breaks/ scattered weed lines at night on Zara Spooks, Pop-Rs, and prop baits. **This pattern seems to work much better on natural inland lakes!***

Spooks catch monster smallies early/late in the day and <u>AT NIGHT!</u>

   A close secondary pattern at night is a large (1/2- to 3/4-ounce) short-arm, single-bladed <u>black spinnerbait</u> with a large Colorado or Indiana blade in <u>copper</u>, <u>red</u>, or <u>black</u> color. Fish the spinnerbait along deep-water break lines!

Chapter 4 Fall Fishing

Most of us look at fall as cooler nights and daytime temperatures followed by the changing of the leaves. To me fall smallmouth fishing begins on September 23rd when autumn begins. About 1 week after the beginning of autumn the bigger smallies begin moving out of deep water to feed on drop-offs, shoals, and flats. They can be taken on a variety of lures and presentations at this time.

The water temps are often in the 60's when this begins. As the fall season continues through October and into November the water temps go down through the 50's and into the 40's. I use water temps in the fall to select the best lure(s) and presentation(s). **The following are my *tips* for fall trophies:**

*Special note: As the water temps decrease in fall some 6-pound plus smallies will come up on the flats to feed (**"power fish" a 3/4-ounce spinnerbait on the flats**). If you are not catching any trophies in shallow water (5 to 12 feet), target deeper water. Beginning at 55°F and downward the biggest smallies start to school together in 30 to 45 feet deep where bladebaits are the best lures to use for the lunkers.*

Water temp: 64°F down to 55°F

Mr Bass Tip #7: My lures at these water temps are: Deep/medium-diving jerkbaits, crankbaits, tubes, lipless crankbaits, spinnerbaits

Presentation: Use a deep-diving suspending jerkbait or a medium-diving suspending jerkbait in natural patterns. Use a small cross-lock snap to allow quick lure changes. Make a long cast back behind the boat and set trolling motor on 40 %. Let more line out, engage the spool and use jerk, jerk, pause; jerk, pause with rod tip held close to water surface. This is a Great Lakes technique called "strolling" (learned from the Pennsylvania boys). Use

8 to 10-pound-test fluorocarbon line to get lure as deep as possible. **TARGET GOOD STRUCTURE AT 15 TO 35 FEET DEEP!**

Special note: *Use "strolling" presentation for deep-diving jerkbaits in 15 to 35 foot depths. <u>Cast</u> medium-diving jerkbaits in 10 to 13 foot depths with same retrieve.*

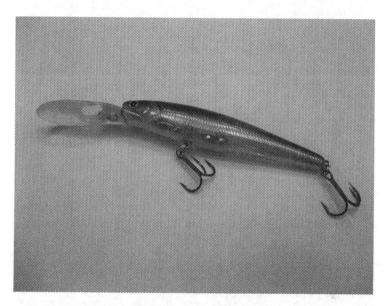

Trophy smallmouth can't turn down deep-diving suspending jerkbaits!

Presentation: *Use <u>medium</u> and/or <u>deep-diving</u> crankbaits in <u>crawdad</u> or <u>shad</u> patterns on 12-pound-test fluorocarbon line. Use erratic retrieve and occasionally bump the lake bottom with the lure.* **TARGET GOOD STRUCTURE AT 10 TO 20 FEET.**

Presentation: *Use 1/2- to 3/4-ounce tube jigs. Use tubes in colors <u>green</u> and <u>brown</u> hues with some <u>red</u>, <u>gold</u> or <u>purple</u> flake. Drift or cast tubes with dragging and/or light shaking presentation.* **TARGET GOOD STRUCTURE AT 20 TO 40 FEET DEEP!**

Presentation: *Use 1/2-ounce lipless crankbait in a <u>chrome</u> finish. Use high-speed reel (7.1:1 & up) and erratic, stop-in-go retrieve. I often replace the factory*

*hooks with high quality round bend hooks. TARGET SCATTERED ROCKS/
BOULDERS, SHOALS AND FLATS AT 7 TO 12 FEET DEEP!*

My favorite; 3/4- ounce spinnerbait with thin blades & trailer hook!

Presentation: Use 1/2- to 3/4-ounce spinnerbait with high-speed reel
(7.1:1 & up) and "power fish" flats with isolated rocks/boulders and break lines
in 7 to 12 feet of water. I like <u>chartreuse/white</u> and <u>shad</u> patterns skirts. My
spinnerbait of choice is a double-willowleaf with "thin" blades for burning the
lure. Blades of various colors and with sparkle are also very effective.

Water temp: 55°F down to 42°F

*Mr Bass Tip #8: My lures at these water temps are: Bladebaits
(best), deep- diving jerkbaits*

Presentation: Use 3/4- to 1-ounce <u>silver</u>, <u>pearl</u>, or <u>gold</u> bladebait. Use a
small cross-lock snap in the center hole (if there are three) on the bladebait. I
usually put high quality split rings and round bend hooks on my bladebaits.
Use 10- to 12-pound-test fluorocarbon line and a vertical presentation. ***<u>Fish
from the lake bottom up six inches. Lift the lure just enough to get
vibration and drop on a semi-tight line.</u>*** The bass usually hits the lure

on the fall or as you begin to lift the bait off the bottom. ***TARGET GOOD STRUCTURE AT 25 TO 45 FEET DEEP!***

Rex caught this 7 lb. 4 oz. trophy in the fall on a bladebait

Bruce with 5-½ pound smallie caught on
5/8- oz. bladebait at 28 feet deep

Presentation: *Use a deep-diving suspending jerkbait in natural patterns. Use a small cross-lock snap to allow quick lure changes. Make a long cast back behind the boat and set trolling motor on 40 %. Let more line out, engage the spool and use jerk, jerk, pause; jerk, pause with rod tip held close to water surface. This is a Great Lakes technique called "strolling" (learned from the Pennsylvania boys). Use 8- to 10-pound-test fluorocarbon line to get lure as deep as possible.* **TARGET GOOD STRUCTURE AT 20 TO 35 FEET DEEP!**

Chapter 5 Winter Fishing

Trophy smallmouth are schooled together in winter by class size. They are often at 25 to 45 feet deep depending on the depth of the lake (if the lake isn't 25 feet deep, look for the deepest water). Curiously they will hold on somewhat flat bottoms with little structure or breaks. You may have to cover a lot of water, but once you find them, they usually stay put.

These schools may contain dozens to hundreds of lunkers. A skilled angler(s) can seriously damage the trophy pool! *Exercise care with landing, handling, and release of these trophy bass!!!*

Water temp: 44°F down to hard water

Mr Bass Tip #9: My lure at these water temps are: Bladebaits (best)

Author with 6 pound 4 ounce smallie caught at 42 feet deep!

**Special note: *Nothing beats a bladebait when
the water temps are in the low 40's!***

Presentation: Use 3/4- to 1-ounce <u>silver</u>, <u>pearl</u>, or <u>gold</u> bladebait. Use a small cross-lock snap in the center hole (if there are three) on the bladebait. I usually put high quality split rings and round bend hooks on my bladebaits. Use 10- to 12-pound-test fluorocarbon line and a vertical presentation. **<u>Fish from the lake bottom up six inches. Lift the lure just enough to get vibration and drop on a semi-tight line.</u>** The bass usually hits the lure on the fall or as you begin to lift the bait off the bottom. **TARGET GOOD STRUCTURE AT 25 TO 45 FEET DEEP!**

Section VII

Summary

SUMMARY

My bass fishing life has been surrounded by many great bass anglers and fishing friends! I have met quite a few and learned a lot from many others such as Buck Perry, Al Lindner, Dough Hannon, Homer Circle, Glen Lau, Roland Martin, and John Weiss. This book is a tribute to all of them.

Any angler dedicated to this endeavor can catch trophy largemouth and smallmouth bass **on purpose***. **Right time, right place, right presentation** is the formula for success!!! This also requires an "attention to detail" and "critical thinking" in everything involved in the process.*

The concepts, tips, pictures, and presentations contained in this book are taken from my own personal experiences in pursuing trophy largemouth and smallmouth bass for over 50 years. Follow the process and you to will put lunkers in the boat! The lure(s) and presentation(s) suggested have been proven and validated by yours truly.

My hope is that you can take from this book and catch that "Bass of a Lifetime". When you do, look me up, as I would love to share that memory with you! Making lifetime memories is what it's all about...

Tight Lines,
James Orr (Mr Bass)

Printed in the United States
By Bookmasters